YOUTH CRIME

Jenny Vaughan

W
FRANKLIN WATTS
LONDON · SYDNEY

First published in 2011 by
Franklin Watts
338 Euston Road
London NW1 3BH

Franklin Watts Australia
Level 17/207 Kent Street
Sydney NSW 2000

Series editor: Jeremy Smith
Editor: Julia Bird
Design: sprout.uk.com
Artworks: sprout.uk.com
Picture researcher: Diana Morris
Consultant: Dr Howard Williamson CBE FRSA,
Professor of European Youth Policy, Faculty of
Humanities and Social Sciences, University of
Glamorgan

A CIP catalogue record for this book is available
from the British Library.

ISBN 978 0 7496 9580 4
Dewey classification: 364.3'6

Printed in China

Franklin Watts is a division of Hachette Children's
Books, an Hachette UK company.
www.hachette.co.uk

Picture credits: Ace Stock/Alamy: front cover cl.
AP/PAI: 32. Marc Asnin/Corbis: 39. Michael Austen/
Alamy: front cover cr. Bettmann/Corbis: 11.
John Birdsall/PAI: 40. British Museum, London/Art
Archive: 10. Burger/Phanie/Rex Features: 38.
Daniel Dempster Photography/Alamy: 41. Lisa
Eastman/istockphoto: 15b. Alex Ekins/Alamy: 26.
Jonathan Hordle/Rex Features: 19. Owen
Humphreys/PA Archive/PAI: 31. Mike Hutchings/
Reuters/Corbis: 25. Image Source/Getty Images: 18.
Image Source Pink/Alamy: front cover b, 5.
Keystone/Getty Images: 30. Keystone USA/ZUMA/
Rex Features: 34. Nathan King/Alamy: 8.
KPA/ZUMA/Rex Features: 35. Robert Landau/Alamy:
17. Lordprice Collection/Alamy: 12. Manchester
Daily Express/Getty Images: 36. Pictorial Press/
Alamy: 29. Olivier Pirard/Rex Features: 37. Steven
Puetzer/Getty Images: 14. RayArtGraphics/Alamy:
15t. Rex Features: 21, 23, 28, 33. Vladimir Rhys/
Getty Images: 24. Oll Scharf/Getty Images: 27. Sipa
Press/Rex Features: 9. Steve Starr/Corbis: 22.
stockex/Alamy: 20. Greg Wood/AFP/Getty Images:
13. World History Archive/Alamy: 16.

INSIDE CRIME

CONTENTS

Inside picture 8

Changing times 10

'Move along, please' 12

Everybody does it! 14

The problem with sex 16

The demon drink 18

Drugs and young people 20

Gangs 22

Case study: Youth gangs
  in South Africa 24

Armed and dangerous 26

Children who kill 28

Case study: The story
  of Mary Bell 30

School and college massacres 32

On trial 34

'Banged up' 36

Alternatives to prison 38

Prevention is better than cure 40

Glossary 42

Further information 43

Index 44

INSIDE PICTURE

'Youth crime' is just that: crime committed by young people. Statistics show that in the USA alone, it accounts for around a fifth of all reported crime. It can be anything from shoplifting to major violence, even murder. It is committed mostly, but not always, by boys and young men, though girls are more often involved than in the past. The only thing that makes it different from other crime is the age of the offenders – but this can greatly affect the way the authorities react to it.

What do they do – and why?

Statistics show that most crimes young people commit fall into two categories: crimes against property (eg burglary and robbery, which account for around 40% of youth crime in the US), and violence. Much goes unreported, especially when it is directed against other young people, who are reluctant to 'tell tales'.

Youth crime is very often simply for gain. Young people steal in order to get things they might not be able to afford. It can also be committed for fun – spray-painting graffiti and other forms of vandalism may fall into this category, as these activities can make ordinary life seem more exciting. Crime may also be a way of venting anger and frustration. In the case of violence, alcohol is often to blame. Drugs too play a part, with some crimes being committed to feed a habit, or while under the influence of drugs.

BUSTED!

Few young criminals have gone as far as a young man from the US. 'Colt' Harris-Moore, known as the 'The Barefoot Burglar' because he reportedly carried out his crimes barefoot, stole, flew and crashed three planes – having already stolen cars and boats. He was arrested nine times before he was 15, and was most recently caught in the Bahamas, in July 2010. He had flown there in a stolen aircraft.

▶ *For some young people painting graffiti is an art. Many disagree, seeing it as ugly vandalism and the graffiti artists as criminals.*

▲ *Young inmates in a Chinese juvenile reformatory take part in a 'psychological education' class. Nearly 20,000 of China's 1.5 million prisoners are under 18.*

FACT FILE

Age of criminal responsibility

Examples of the age of criminal responsibility in various countries:

- United States: varies from state to state. Only 13 states have set minimum ages, which range from 6 to 12 years old. The rest rely on 'common law' (experience from past cases) and mostly set the age at around 7.

- Scotland: 8 (but no one under 12 can be tried in an adult court).

- England, Wales, Northern Ireland, South Africa and Australia: 10 (in Australia there are extra safeguards between 10 and 14 which aim to make sure the child knows that he or she has done wrong).

- India, Nigeria, Canada, Japan, the Netherlands and Turkey: 12

- France, Greece and Poland: 13

- China, Russia, Italy, Romania, Latvia, Hungary and Germany: 14

- Norway, Sweden, Denmark, the Czech Republic and Slovakia: 15

- Most of Spain and Portugal: 16

- Belgium: 18 (16 for serious offences).

Criminal responsibility

In most countries, there is an age below which children are thought to be too young to understand that they have committed a crime (see Fact File). This is called the 'age of criminal responsibility'. It varies between countries, and even states – it can be anything from seven or eight years old to 16 or even 18. After that age, there can be several categories of 'youth' – ranging from the youngest children through to 'juveniles' (usually between 15 and 18) and 'young offenders' (between 18 and 21).

Sentencing

An offender's age reflects the type of sentence he or she receives. In most countries, young offenders, such as under-18s, are less likely than older ones to be sent to any sort of prison. If they are sentenced at all, it will often be for a shorter period of time than adults, sometimes only half as long. Young offenders are usually held in special accommodation, where the aim is, in theory at least, to provide an education and steer young people away from a life of crime.

CHANGING TIMES

Throughout most of history, young people – even very young children – were seen as simply miniature adults, to be treated as adults, and punished in the same way adults were when they did something wrong. For a long time, there was no real concept of youth crime as being different from any other kind of crime.

Industrialisation

The late 18th century saw the beginning of the period known as the Industrial Revolution, which started in Britain and spread throughout Europe and North America. Huge numbers of people flocked to towns, often living in appalling poverty while working in the newly-built factories. Large numbers of young people, whose parents had either died or were simply unable to look after them, drifted into life on the streets. Many had to steal to survive, and were frequently exploited by adult criminals, who forced them into begging and prostitution.

Harsh punishment

Today, we can understand that these extreme pressures on young people were almost bound to lead them to break the law, but at the beginning of this period of industrialisation, young criminals could not expect much in the way of special treatment. For example, up to 20,000 young people were transported to Australia from the UK between 1787 and 1858. As with adults at the time, this was often for what we would think of as very petty crimes, such as stealing a loaf of bread.

▼ *The 'First Fleet' of ships carrying settlers from Britain to Australia set sail in May 1787. Among the convicts was 13-year-old Elizabeth Hayward, one of the youngest people ever to be transported. She had stolen a dress.*

The New York House of Refuge on Randall's Island, New York, was the United States' first juvenile reformatory.

Houses of Refuge

The family breakdown that came with the Industrial Revolution meant that society took on some of the responsibility of disciplining young criminals. 'Houses of Refuge' were set up in the US and the UK in the 19th century to offer young criminals work and basic education. But in reality they were little better than adult prisons. Social reformers campaigned to replace them with reform schools where better education, and a better environment, could be used to help to steer young offenders away from a life of crime.

Changing attitudes

By the early 20th century, criminal justice systems took more interest in young criminals. It became clear that there should be special youth justice procedures to take offenders' age and maturity into account. The first juvenile courts in the US were set up in Illinois at the start of the 20th century. They were officially established in the UK in 1908.

ON TARGET

In 2009, magistrates in Norwich, in the east of England, marked the setting up of juvenile courts just over 100 years earlier by re-enacting a case from its archives – the 1909 trial of George Walters, aged 13. George had stolen a gold watch in a street robbery, and was sent to a reformatory for three years. The re-enactment aimed to show people how harsh youth justice was in the past, and how far we have progressed in the last 100 years.

'MOVE ALONG, PLEASE'

As long ago as the reign of Edward II of England (1284–1327), there is recorded disapproval of unruly gatherings of youths when the king tried to ban games of medieval football in the hope that the players would do something useful, such as practise archery, instead.

▲ *Medieval football was violent and had almost no rules. It was played on town and village streets, causing huge amounts of damage.*

Hanging about

In many towns and cities, it is common for the police to try to break up groups of young people gathering in public places. The suspicion is that, if left to themselves, young people will probably cause trouble. In some cases they do, and in some they don't, but the police have no real way of knowing. So they tell any young people they suspect to 'move on' or risk being arrested for public order offences. They also stop and search more young people than older ones on suspicion of being involved in some crimes, such as drug dealing or carrying an illegal weapon.

BUSTED!

The beautiful city of Bath in England depends on tourism for much of its income. The authorities there have decided to get tough on rowdy young people. In the spring of 2009, three teenage girls were sentenced to youth custody from eight to ten months for 'public order offences' and a 13-year-old boy was banned from certain areas of the city. 'We will not tolerate bad behaviour. We want these young people to have a good time, but not at the expense of other people coming in to the city to have a nice night out,' said a local police chief.

Stopping and searching can make older people feel more comfortable, but adults who work with young people worry that this drives them into out-of-the-way places where they may come under the influence of more serious trouble-makers. Resentment against the police builds up, too.

'Picking on us'

Young people who are constantly the subject of police interest can feel they are being harassed. When racial tensions add to this mix, the result can be explosive. This was the case in November 2005, in a poor suburb of Paris, France. Two youths of African origin died after being accidentally electrocuted as they were running away from the police. Nearly three weeks of riots followed, causing millions of pounds' worth of damage. Nearly 3,000 young people were arrested, about 300 police and firefighters injured, and one passerby was killed.

Similar riots have happened in other cities where tensions have grown up between the police and groups of angry young people. In 2004 in Redfern, a suburb of Sydney, Australia, an Aboriginal Australian youth called Thomas Hickey (TJ) impaled himself on railings after fleeing from a police car. He later died from his injuries. An angry mob gathered, blaming the police for Hickey's death. Tensions quickly escalated when youths threw bricks and bottles at the police, and a full-scale riot ensued.

▶ A young girl takes part in a protest march in memory of teenager, Thomas Hickey, who died in February 2004 after a police chase.

EVERYBODY DOES IT!

When people break the law – whether they are young or old – they often like to make excuses for themselves. They may try to make their crimes seem unimportant, saying things like 'But everybody does it', or 'What I did doesn't hurt anyone'. Criminologists call excuses like these 'vocabularies of motive'. When young people discuss the crimes they commit, they very often use these kind of terms.

What's the problem?

Some crimes are so common that many who commit them hardly think of them as illegal at all. Fare-dodging on public transport, for example, seems to be victimless. Small-scale shoplifting might seem reasonably harmless, while illegally downloading music appears to hurt no one except wealthy music companies. Using some kinds of 'soft' drugs and under-age drinking are commonplace in some communities, where few young people take them very seriously.

ON TARGET

The state of South Australia has an unusual way of tackling shoplifting. A law passed in 2000 means that shoplifters can be made to do one hour's community service for every 5 dollars' (£3) worth of goods stolen.

Other, more serious crimes, especially among young people, are rarely reported because the victims can be afraid of the consequences of making the crimes public. These crimes can include bullying other young people to the point of hurting them, or even stealing from them.

Laws for a reason

In reality, few crimes are victimless. The more people shoplift, the more others must pay to make up the costs to the company. In the UK a fifth of all shoplifting is carried out by under-18s, and costs shops around £120 million a year. When music is illegally downloaded, the band that made it and the music company that produced it are deprived of the income they need to go on making music.

◄ Shoplifting may seem victimless, but it is still theft and can undermine a shop's business.

BUSTED!

In Hamburg in Germany, in October 2010, a trial of a young man accused of illegally downloading and sharing music came to an end after five years. The man, aged 16 when the trial started, was fined only 30 Euros (£25), but only because there were just two songs involved and both were old. But he was lucky. By contrast, around the same time, a woman in the US was asked to pay $1.5 million in damages for downloading and sharing 24 songs.

▲ A young man smokes a hand-rolled 'joint' of cannabis – also called marijuana. In some communities, the use of this drug is widespread, but possession is usually illegal and can lead to a criminal record.

Drinking and smoking

Crimes involving drink and drugs are also against the law for a reason. Alcohol is a powerful substance, and is harmful to young people (see pages 18–19.) The law is there to protect them, as it is with drugs. Even drugs that seem reasonably harmless, such as marijuana, can have damaging long-term effects.

Criminal record

Committing a crime can result in punishment and a criminal record. Illegally downloading music in the US state of Massachusetts can lead to a prison sentence, or a fine of thousands of dollars. A criminal record stays on a person's records for years and can limit opportunities – in education, travel and study, for example.

▼ Downloading music files illegally can lead to a fine and a criminal record.

THE PROBLEM WITH SEX

In most countries, there are laws about the age at which young people may have sex. These make it illegal for anyone to have sex with anyone under a certain age, known as the age of consent. In most countries, this is around age 16. These laws are designed to protect young people from being exploited.

Why is it illegal?

In Victorian England child prostitution was commonplace, as it is still in some parts of the world today. Young girls, barely in their teens, could be bought, sold and exported all over Europe to work in brothels. Campaigners tried to bring this scandal to public attention, but the issue did

FACT FILE

- In many countries, parents who allow their children to have under-age sex may be prosecuted.

- Having sex with someone who is under the age of consent is always regarded as rape in some countries, whether or not the young person agreed to it. Elsewhere, there is a younger age that automatically assumes the child has been raped. In the UK, this is 13.

- Homosexuality is sometimes subject to different laws from heterosexual sex. In many countries, it is completely illegal, while in others, the age of consent is higher than for heterosexual (male and female) couples.

not hit the headlines until a journalist, William Stead, described how he had managed to buy a 13-year-old girl from her mother, pretending he was going to use her for prostitution. Today, we often read about adults who seek sexual relationships with children – through the Internet and in other ways. It is they, rather than the children, who are criminals.

◀ *In Victorian times, the age of consent was just 13. The work of campaigning journalist William Stead (left) resulted in the age of consent being raised in 1885 to 16.*

'Romeo and Juliet'

However, the issue of under-age sex becomes complicated when there seems to be no question of exploitation. It is, after all, possible for an under-age person to put pressure on someone who is over the age of consent to have sex. In doing so, they are encouraging their partner to break the law. The law, strictly speaking, may also apply when a 16-year-old has sex with a willing partner close to them in age. In practice, in most countries, no one would be arrested, and in some, such as Canada, this is actually spelled out in law. (This is called the 'Romeo and Juliet Law', after Shakespeare's play about two young lovers.) Under-age people can still commit the crime of rape though.

Conflicting attitudes

Whatever the law says, adult attitudes to young sex tend to be confused. Many try to encourage young people to postpone sex until they are at least in their late teens, when they are likely to be better able to handle any risks it may bring to their emotions and their health. Yet, at the same time, young people are surrounded by images of sex, and sexy, 'adult' clothing is often on sale to very young girls.

ON TARGET

There is evidence that good sex education encourages young people to delay their first experience of sex, which can help to protect them from being exploited. In the Netherlands, sex education begins in primary school, with an emphasis on love and commitment. The average age for first sexual experience there is nearly 18 (compared with 16 in the UK and the US). The Netherlands also has one of the lowest rates of teen pregnancy in the world – though some experts say that public attitudes to family life and to single parenthood may affect this as much as sex education.

▶ Young people are bombarded with highly sexualised images through advertising.

THE DEMON DRINK

Alcohol can be a dangerous and addictive drug, responsible for a lot of crime, as well as deaths through disease and as a result of accidents. Yet, for many, drinking alcohol in moderation is a normal, socially acceptable occurrence.

Binge drinking

Because of the problems alcohol can cause, most governments try to stop young people drinking it until they reach a certain age, when it is hoped they are old enough to use alcohol sensibly. This age varies: in the US, it is 21; elsewhere it is usually younger – around 18. It is widely recognised that, although people of all ages may drink too much, there is a special problem with the young. This is 'heavy episodic drinking', also called 'binge drinking'.

Drink driving

Driving under the influence of alcohol is a crime. It especially affects young people because they are likely to be less experienced both as drivers and drinkers, and cannot judge what alcohol is doing to them. Alcohol slows down reactions, making it harder to stop quickly, reduces the driver's ability to see clearly and, at the same time, makes the driver feel over-confident. In the US, it is estimated that around 20% fewer lives are lost each year as a direct result of laws that make it illegal for under-21s to drink.

▼ *Even a small amount of alcohol can slow down reactions and impair judgement, which makes driving very dangerous. Around 20–30% of road accidents are believed to be caused by binge drinking.*

Drinking and fighting

Drinking lowers self-control and can therefore sometimes lead to violence. Surveys in many countries show that alcohol-related violence is highest among young people, increasing throughout teenage years and peaking just before or during the early 20s. In Finland, for example, nearly half of all reported violent incidents among people aged 12 to 18 involved alcohol.

The big picture

Alcohol also plays a large part in domestic violence, as well as damage to property, driving offences, stealing cars and much more. It impairs judgement and self-control – which can easily lead to underage and unprotected sex. This in turn has serious consequences to health. In addition to all that, the costs of alcohol-linked crime are enormous, running into billions of pounds paid out in healthcare, legal fees and time lost from work.

The US National Institute on Alcohol Abuse and Alcoholism estimates that, each year, alcohol abuse costs the US around $185 billion.

◀ *A young man sits slumped on the pavement after a night's drinking. Bouts of heavy 'binge drinking' like this can lead to accidents and illness, as well as crime.*

ON TARGET

Making it harder for young people to get hold of alcohol can significantly reduce violent crime. One way to do this is to make alcohol expensive. It is estimated that a 10% increase in the price of beer could bring down violence among college students by 4%. In Brazil, it is estimated that ending alcohol sales after 11pm has helped prevent nearly 300 murders (among all ages) over two years.

DRUGS AND YOUNG PEOPLE

Research in the US shows that the peak time for using illegal drugs for the first time starts in the late teens. When people use the term 'drugs' they usually mean a wide range of substances, including ecstasy, cocaine, heroin and cannabis – the last being most widely used. The problems drugs cause include damage to health and family life. Addiction can also lead young people into a life of crime.

The risks

Young people are especially vulnerable to drug use. The world of drug-taking may seem exciting and adult, and there is often plenty of peer pressure to encourage it. However, drugs are illegal because they cause risks to health. Although there are many arguments about which drugs are the most dangerous, it is true in most countries that using drugs means you are breaking the law. Depending on the country you are in, which drugs you take, and in many cases whether or not you are dealing rather than just using drugs, the result can be that you end up in prison. In a few countries, such as Iran and Thailand, the death penalty may be used.

FACT FILE

Cannabis

The most widely used illegal drug in the world is cannabis, also known as marijuana. There is debate about how harmful it is. In the US – where it is estimated that over 40% of people have used it at some time in their lives – it is classed alongside heroin as one of the most dangerous drugs. In other countries, including the UK, its use is considered slightly less serious. However, there are fears that stronger strains can be extremely dangerous, and many anti-drug campaigners believe its use can be a first step to other, more harmful drugs.

◀ *A young man buys illegal drugs from a dealer. Young drug addicts can get drawn into crime to support their costly habit.*

Addiction

Drug dealers need buyers and highly addictive drugs, such as heroin and cocaine, give them a ready source of customers for years. Young people whose lives are chaotic and problematic are especially vulnerable. They may soon find themselves drawn into a whole range of crimes, both because they are under the influence of drugs, and because they need money to pay for a habit.

Lured into a life of crime

There is a close link between the drug trade and organised crime, and it is all too easy for young people to become involved. Dealers will often use young people to distribute the drugs, as they are less likely to suffer serious penalties if they are caught. The young people themselves are attracted to the trade because of the money it offers.

▼ *These pictures from an anti-drug campaign show the damaging effects of just four years' use of the dangerously addictive drug methamphetamine (crystal meth).*

ON TARGET

All over the world, governments try to find ways to convince young people to stay away from drugs. An example of this is a Facebook Fanpage (www.facebook.com/drugsnot4me), launched in August 2010 by Health Canada, a Canadian government agency, as part of a youth drug prevention campaign.

The page gives information about the different illegal drugs young people are likely to come across, as well as giving young people a place where they can share their thoughts on the harmful effects of drugs.

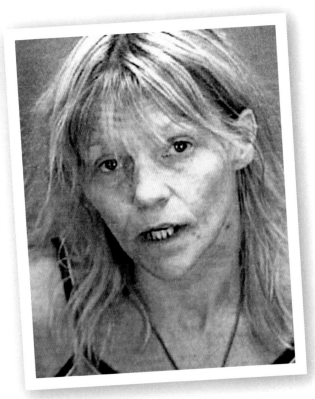

GANGS

What is a gang? There is no clear definition – the word can mean anything from a group of friends to an organised crime syndicate. Mostly, it means 'street gangs' of young people who identify themselves as gang members. There is usually no law against membership – only against the crimes that some youth gangs commit, such as carrying illegal weapons, stealing cars, burglary, robbery, dealing in drugs and often, linking up with adult organised crime.

Gangs past and present

Street gangs have been around for a long time. Some have existed over years, drawing in new members as older ones drift away. Examples include the 'Crips' and 'Bloods' rival gangs in Los Angeles, USA, infamous for violence and murder, which grew up in the 1960s, and still exist today. Gangs are found in cities all over the world. In many ways they are similar, often claiming neighbourhoods as 'theirs', and carrying weapons.

Who joins a gang?

If there is such a thing as a typical gang, it is made up of a few older people at the top of the hierarchy, who are involved in serious organised crime, such as the drugs trade. A younger group of boys and, increasingly, girls, may also take part in violent crime. An even younger group will be 'hangers on' who run errands, hide weapons and so on. These are the 'foot-soldiers' – employed to do the day-to-day work of the gang (such as delivering drugs), because they are less likely to arouse suspicion than older members and, if they are caught, less likely to be severely punished.

◄ *Young 'Crips' gang members from Los Angeles wait in a doorway – their faces partly covered and a gun at the ready.*

A new family

Young people who are drawn into gangs often have chaotic home lives, with parents who have their own problems. With no boundaries set at home, and no proper adult guidance, gang membership can offer something like a substitute family, bringing respect and protection. Yet joining a gang can be, as one criminologist describes it, 'an escalator, taking young people to a new and more serious level of criminal involvement'.

Warfare

Gang activity can affect whole neighbourhoods. Older people find gangs intimidating and young people who are not in gangs live in fear of them. Rivalry over issues such as territory can turn violent. Many gang members have been stabbed or shot because someone decided they were in the wrong part of town. Occasionally, non-gang members die when they are mistaken for rivals, or simply get caught in crossfire.

ON TARGET

In Central America there are violent street gangs called 'maras'. In September 2010, a law was signed by the President of El Salvador making 'mara' membership illegal, with penalties of up to ten years in prison. Critics say that tough anti-gang laws are not the solution. Instead, they want improvements in the justice system, along with more jobs, better education and healthcare, to tackle the reasons why young people join gangs. They also criticise the fact that the law treats very young gang members in the same way as adults.

BUSTED!

In the UK in December 2008, Sean Mercer (seen below) was given a life sentence for murdering 11-year-old Rhys Jones in August 2007 when Mercer was just 16. Rhys was on his way home from football practice. Mercer was a member of a violent street gang that called itself the Croxteth Young Guns gang. They were involved in a violent rivalry with a gang from a neighbouring area, and Rhys, it turned out, was killed by mistake.

▲ In 2007, gang member Sean Mercer shot and killed 11-year-old Rhys Jones. He was convicted of murder the following year.

CASE STUDY: YOUTH GANGS IN SOUTH AFRICA

South Africa has a long history of gangs and violent crime, particularly amongst the youth in its 'townships' – poor suburbs and shanty-towns. Young people are especially important in South Africa as, as is the case in many parts of the developing world, they make up a huge proportion of the population. One third of South Africa's population is under 16, compared with only a fifth in the US.

Family breakdown

In 1948, a new government came into power in South Africa, and set in place a system of government known as 'apartheid'. This became more extreme over the following years. It gave the best of everything to the minority white population, while non-whites lived in varying degrees of poverty. The system, which dictated where people should live and what jobs they could do, destroyed traditional extended families. It also meant that parents frequently had to work and live apart from their children and each other. Those that did live together often did so in extreme poverty.

Criminal traditions

The role of the police during the apartheid years was primarily to enforce the system. The majority of the non-white population treated them with suspicion, and certainly did not look to them for protection. The townships became lawless places. 'Tsotsis' – the black urban gangsters that had been around since the 1930s – grew in power. Generations of children were drawn towards gangs. Some were following in their families' footsteps, others, who were left drifting on to the streets as their own immediate families fell apart, found them irresistible. Gangs provided alternative families and support networks.

◀ Teenagers from a South African township. The apartheid system of government in South Africa left a legacy of extreme poverty. Many young boys turn to gang life to make money.

▲ *Former South African gang member Magadien Wentzel. Wentzel spent 25 years in a gang called the 28s. He now campaigns for social reform.*

Children without parents

Today, although apartheid in South Africa has ended, poverty and poor education and services remain for the vast majority of people. Now, a new problem has arrived. This is the AIDS epidemic that, in 2007 alone, killed 300,000 South Africans – nearly 1,000 a day. That year, there were an estimated 1.4 million AIDS orphans created, many of whom had to fend for themselves on the streets. For these youngsters, like their predecessors, gang life offers a tempting alternative family.

What can be done?

Many campaigners believe that putting more and more people – especially young ones – behind bars as a way of combating crime only makes South Africa's youth crime problems worse. Instead, they say, it is important to concentrate on supporting young people, and working with them to steer them away from gang life.

ON TARGET

South Africans are developing a number of organisations in which ordinary people can play a part in tackling the high level of youth crime. Proudly Manenberg, a non-governmental organisation in a township just outside Cape Town, was set up by a group of people who were once anti-apartheid activists, and who now want to see their home town change for the better. One way they are doing this is by raising money to give people more opportunities, especially in education. This, they hope will help 'suffocate' the gangs that so attract young people by depriving them of the space they need to operate.

ARMED AND DANGEROUS

For some young people, carrying a weapon is a way of life. They may see a weapon as security, protection or simply a means of earning social status or 'respect'. Sadly, carrying weapons does not keep young people safe. Every year in Europe, 6,000 or so young people are stabbed to death.

Which weapons?

Knives tend to be used by young people rather than guns, as in most countries there are strict rules about who can buy or carry firearms. Even in the US, where many states have comparatively relaxed laws about carrying guns, nearly all states forbid it for under-18s. That does not mean, of course, that young people cannot get hold of guns. In 2005, firearm homicide was the second highest cause of death among 15- to 24-year-olds in the US (after accidents), and although the UK has some of the strictest gun control rules in the world, there are cities where people – especially young people – can, and do, carry guns.

▼ *Young people often think that carrying a weapon will help keep them safe from gang members and bullies. In fact, they are actually putting themselves in greater danger.*

FACT FILE

This is UK government advice to young people who are tempted to carry a knife. What do you think?

By carrying a knife you:
- are giving yourself a false sense of security;
- could be arming your attacker (if he or she gets hold of the knife), increasing the risk of getting stabbed or injured;
- are breaking the law.

Not carrying, and walking away from confrontation:
- is what the vast majority do;
- is the tougher thing to do;
- means you'll be safer from serious harm and not breaking the law.

How many and why?

It is hard to know how many young people carry weapons, as few are likely to admit to it. One survey in the UK in 2004 suggested that 9% of 11- to 16-year-olds in school had carried a flick-knife at some time in the previous year, while 30% of excluded

ON TARGET

In the United States, the issue of owning guns is controversial, and many people believe everyone should have the right to own one. There are an estimated 200 million privately-held guns in the US and, according to one survey, half of all high school students claim that they could get hold of one if they really wanted to. However, the freedom to own and carry firearms is restricted. One restriction is age – no one under 18 may own a gun and, in publicly-funded schools, any student who brings a firearm to school must be expelled for at least a year.

pupils had done so. Many also admitted to carrying kitchen knives. A recent survey in the US suggested that nearly a quarter of boys had carried a weapon of some kind (including a gun) in the past month. Some experts believe that weapons are mainly status symbols, but most young people claim that they carry them for self-defence.

False security

However, the idea that carrying a weapon can make a young person safer is the opposite of the truth. It actually increases the danger. A senior police spokesperson reports: 'People give all sorts of reasons why they carry knives, including protecting themselves. But a knife is not a weapon of defence, it's a weapon of offence.' (Karyn McCluskey, Metropolitan Police, London.)

▲ A 'knife scanner', set up by London's Metropolitan Police in a shopping centre. It is a mobile metal-detector designed to catch anyone who is carrying a knife.

CHILDREN WHO KILL

Following the Industrial Revolution of the late 18th and early 19th centuries (see pages 10–11), people began to develop a new view of childhood. Children were seen as essentially innocent and in need of protection. This view persists today – and, as a result, the idea of one child killing another seems quite unnatural. The media goes along with this, so when children are violent and dangerous, they are seen as something strangely and exceptionally evil – as 'monsters'.

A special horror

In 1993 two-year-old James Bulger, from Liverpool, was abducted and beaten to death by two 10-year-olds, Robert Thompson and Jon Venables. Public reaction was extreme. A crowd formed outside the court where the boys were on trial, and the van bringing them to the trial was stoned. Inside the court, there was massive media interest: the press covered every moment of the trial in detail, describing the boys as evil, and demanding vengeance.

The trial

When the judge sentenced Thompson and Venables to a minimum of eight years in detention there was another outcry, and several attempts were made to lengthen their sentence. Seventeen years later, when Jon Venables was re-arrested on a different charge, the outcry was repeated. Some commentators have said that it was as if the very young age of the killers actually made the public demand a greater punishment for them than if they had been adults.

▲ One of the most dramatic aspects of the killing of James Bulger was the CCTV coverage of the little boy being led away by his killers. These pictures quickly led to their arrest.

Less extreme

The following year, there was a very different reaction to a case in Trondheim, Norway. Five-year-old Silje Raedergard was beaten unconscious by three six-year-old boys she had been playing with, and left to die in the snow. Press coverage of the case was far less sensational. Serious attempts were made to find out how and why the tragedy had happened. The boys involved were never publicly named, never charged, and eventually returned to the local kindergarten. Of course, there are differences between the two cases – particularly in the ages of the children – but the lack of media furore and more in-depth attempts to find out what caused the tragedy allowed the young boys in Trondheim to gradually return to a normal life.

Motivation

Why do some children kill? We can usually only guess. Commenting on the Bulger case, a leading child psychiatrist, Dr Dora Black criticised the terms used in the media, and said that she felt the responsibility lay with adults: 'the terms 'evil' and 'monster' are not psychiatric diagnoses. I think children vary in ... how well they have been taught to behave, curb their impulses and how to ... feel for others.'

The writer Gitta Sereny, in a book about another child murderer, Mary Bell (see pages 30–31) seems to agree. She claims that when children kill, this is a sign of deep unhappiness, 'created by the adults they 'belong to'.'

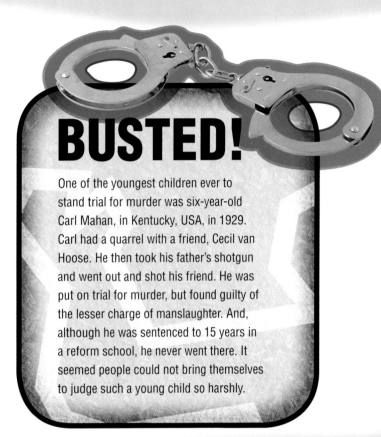

BUSTED!

One of the youngest children ever to stand trial for murder was six-year-old Carl Mahan, in Kentucky, USA, in 1929. Carl had a quarrel with a friend, Cecil van Hoose. He then took his father's shotgun and went out and shot his friend. He was put on trial for murder, but found guilty of the lesser charge of manslaughter. And, although he was sentenced to 15 years in a reform school, he never went there. It seemed people could not bring themselves to judge such a young child so harshly.

▶ A still from Heavenly Creatures, a film about a murder in the early 1950s in New Zealand. Teenagers Pauline Parker and Juliet Hulme killed Pauline's mother, whom they believed wanted to break up their obsessive friendship. The judge said he believed that 'some perversity of the mental process' led them to 'commit the act'.

CASE STUDY: THE STORY OF MARY BELL

The case of Mary Bell is one of the best-known stories of a child who killed. It happened in 1968, in Scotswood, a poor area of Newcastle-on-Tyne, in north-east England. The case and Mary's trial later that year made headlines all over the world.

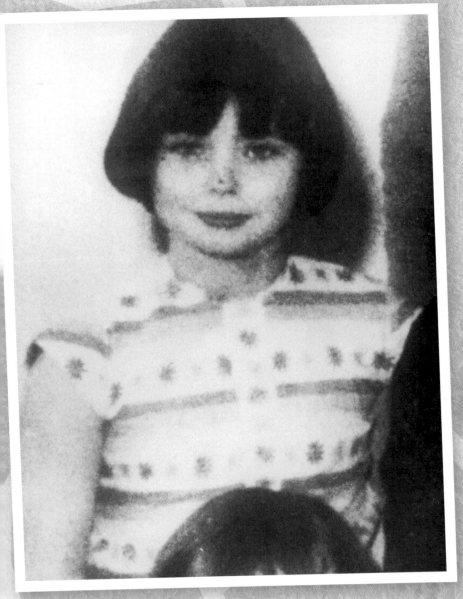

◄ *Mary Bell, aged 11 – around the time of her trial.*

The story

That summer, Mary, then aged 11, strangled two small boys – four-year-old Martin Brown and three-year-old Brian Howe. Afterwards, she behaved strangely, giving hints in writing and pictures that she was guilty. But the police were at first reluctant to believe that a young girl could be responsible.

The trial

Mary and a friend (who was later acquitted) were tried in an adult court. In an attempt to make the trial less frightening, the girls were allowed to sit near their lawyers, instead of in the dock, like adult prisoners. Observers of the trial were astonished at how calm and clear-thinking Mary seemed to be. She was clearly very intelligent and articulate, but she seemed to have no sense of guilt at what she had done. Eventually, she was judged to be dangerously disturbed and found guilty of manslaughter (less serious than murder) on the grounds of 'diminished responsibility'.

Afterwards

After the trial, the authorities had difficulty in knowing what to do with Mary. She was sent to several 'secure units', including a special school where she was the only girl, and later to prison. After 12 years, she was released and given a new name. The media was forbidden to identify her, partly because it was felt that she should not continue to suffer for a crime she had committed when she was so young, and later to protect her young daughter.

▲ The mother of Martin Brown, one of Mary Bell's young victims, holding a photo of her son,

Conclusions

Since 1968, it has become clearer that Mary's background played a huge part in turning her into that rare and frightening phenomenon – a child killer. Stories of extreme neglect and abuse at the hands of adults, particularly her mother, became public knowledge in 1998, when Mary helped author Gitta Sereny write a book called *Cries Unheard* about her life. There was outrage that Mary was profiting from her crimes, but Mary herself apparently thought that telling the whole story was more important than the money she received from sales of the book.

ON TARGET

Mary, and the boys who killed James Bulger, were given new identities after their trials. This was partly to protect them from anyone seeking vengeance, and also in the hope that the young people concerned could rebuild their lives, without always having to live in the shadow of crimes committed while they were so young. They must, it was thought, be given a second chance.

SCHOOL AND COLLEGE MASSACRES

On 21 March 2005, in Red Lake, Minnesota, USA 16-year-old Jeff Weise shot dead his grandfather and his grandfather's partner before heading for his school, Red Lake High. There he shot a teacher, a security guard and five other students. He then shot himself.

◀ Jeff Weise in an undated family photograph. Few, if any, people recognised how disturbed Weise was – in fact many of his fellow students simply described him as 'quiet'.

Not so unusual

The shooting at Red Lake High was one of many school shootings in recent years and the second in Minnesota within 18 months. Many such shootings have been in the US, but they have also happened in several other countries, including Finland, Canada, Germany, Hungary, Sweden, the Netherlands and Australia. Not all involved very young students, but most gunmen (and they were nearly all men), were teenagers or people in their early 20s. Some were as young as 14.

Planning

Many plan their killing sprees. Jeff Weise left clues on his computer, including homemade cartoons about shootings. Similarly, in 2007, 18-year-old Pekka-Eric Auvinen from Finland posted a YouTube video announcing detailed plans for shootings he carried out at his school. Dylan Klebold and Eric Harris, the teenagers responsible for the Columbine school massacre in Colorado, USA in 1999, drew up plans to bomb a student cafeteria, killing around 500 students. These failed, but the two students went on to kill 15 people and injure 23 others.

Why?

Often, the killers are shot by the police, or kill themselves before anyone can ask them why they have killed. But the young killers sometimes leave records of their thoughts, often showing extreme rage; resentment of other students, who they consider less intelligent than themselves; of the school; at being 'left out' or ignored, or bullied. This builds up into an all-consuming anger at the school and fellow students.

After the Red Lake shootings, psychologist David Walsh said he believed that violence in our culture, especially violent television images, amount to 'scripts' that become 'wired' into disturbed young people's brains. Other experts believe there is a genetic component, which makes it easy for an unhappy young person to be 'tipped over the edge'. The reason why the shootings are especially common in the US has been blamed on the country's 'frontier' tradition, of the lone cowboy in the Wild West. But the truth is probably simply that it is easier to buy guns in the United States than in many other countries.

ON TARGET

In May 2010, Christopher Franko, aged 17 and Dana Saltzman, 16, from Long Island, USA were arrested for planning an attack on their school, Connetquot High School. They had apparently spent weeks looking at bomb-making websites and had sent text messages about killing people. It is claimed that Franko was planning to buy shotguns on June 8, his 18th birthday, and carry out the attacks the following day.

▼ Pekka-Eric Auvinen (see p.32) killed eight people at his high school in Jokela, Finland, before shooting himself. These pictures are taken from an online 'manifesto' he made, warning of what he was going to do.

HUMANITY IS OVERRATED

ON TRIAL

Over the last 100 years or so, many countries have set up special juvenile courts to deal with young people who break the law. Until then, it was normal for young people always to be tried in the same way as adults. These special courts tend to be less formal than adult courts, with judges or magistrates who have been specially trained in dealing with young people. They often have a strong welfare element.

Juvenile courts

Different countries – and even different states within the US – all have different ways of putting young people on trial. Much depends on the age of criminal responsibility (see pages 8–9). Below that age, young people are not dealt with by the courts at all, and if they do something that would be a crime if they were older, it is a matter for the welfare authorities.

In most countries, juvenile courts (called 'youth courts' in the UK and 'children's courts' in Australia) are in theory, at least, meant to help young people as much as to punish them. However, there can be confusion about their role, and which is more important – punishment or welfare.

Juvenile to adult

In some countries and some US states, very serious crimes committed by anyone over the age of criminal responsibility must be referred to adult courts after the first hearing in a court for young people. This means that children as young as 10 or 11 in the UK or Australia may be tried in an adult court. (This is more likely to be 13 in the United States.) Many campaigners believe this is inappropriate, and should be changed so that children are not faced with intimidating courtrooms and procedures which they may not understand.

▼ Juvenile defendants await trial in a US juvenile court. Their identities are concealed because of their youth.

Punishment

When it comes to actually punishing young people, in most countries, sentences are much lighter than for adults and there may be a strong welfare element. In the Netherlands, for example, around half the children in youth detention will be there for the treatment of mental health problems. By contrast, in the US, when young people are tried in adult courts, they are usually given adult punishments – so that in some states someone as young as 12 may be sentenced to life without parole for murder. (The death penalty, still used in some US states, cannot be given to anyone under 18.)

▶ 15-year-old Tylar Witt, from California, USA, will be tried as an adult for her part in the murder of her mother in June 2010, and could face life in prison if found guilty. If she had been tried as a juvenile she would have been eligible for release at age 25.

ON TARGET

A court appearance can be traumatic for a young person, and in some countries, the authorities try hard to avoid it. In Sweden and Denmark, for example, under-15s cannot be prosecuted at all. Instead, if they commit criminal acts, they are considered 'troubled', and are the responsibility of the welfare system. Even over-15s may be kept out of court, if that seems to be in their best interests. 'Diversion' (getting the young person to admit guilt and to make restitution) may be used instead of a trial, and prosecution may be dropped in favour of a welfare package.

'BANGED UP'

In many places, including some states in the US, young people are routinely put in adult prisons where they can be subject to the same conditions and treatment as adult prisoners. However, in most developed countries, they are sent instead to special facilities for young offenders, such as secure children's homes and young offenders' institutes.

Punishment or education?

Some experts believe there is the same public confusion around these juvenile facilities as there is around courts for young people. Are they meant to help young people, or primarily to punish them? This uncertainty means life there can vary. Some institutions do their best to help young people, by offering useful education, care, psychiatric help and support. In others, by contrast, overcrowding and poor facilities make them more like adult prisons, where inmates are often deeply unhappy, bullied

and frightened. Such regimes can lead inmates to self-harm or even suicide. There is also the risk that they will learn from their tougher, more experienced companions, adding to the risk that they will leave as hardened, angry, young (potential) criminals.

Limited resources

Many young people who end up in prison are disturbed and often have drink and drug problems. The adults working with them know that they need help at least as much as punishment – and without help they will almost certainly offend again. They know too that the young people who end up in institutions have often failed at

▼ Offenders at a 'borstal' in England in 1969. The first of these institutions for young male offenders aged 16–21 opened in 1902, and they offered work and education, along with strict discipline.

▲ *Young offenders in Belgium in a woodworking class in a centre that seeks to rehabilitate the young people by offering sport and practical activities.*

school, and are badly in need of education. But finding the time, money and other resources to meet all these needs can be difficult.

Making a change?

According to research, the majority of young people in detention find themselves back in trouble within two years. Some pressure groups argue that harsh treatment should warn them off re-offending. Others think that looking at why young people get into trouble in the first place is a better solution. They say that because so many have failed at school, education can help, along with support in finding employment on release. Drug and alcohol treatment can reduce re-offending by around 11%. Figures show that 'Offending behaviour programmes' to help to change the way young people think and show them how to avoid situations which lead to law-breaking can also cut reoffending by 14%.

ON TARGET

The Scandinavian countries are famous for their very liberal approach to crime, but even by their standards, the Hassela Reform Centre, in Sweden is extraordinary. It houses 60 'students' – young people with criminal records, or a history of anti-social behaviour, or drug problems. The centre, which is run by two teachers, tries to replicate family life for the young people who are sent there, as well as to give them training opportunities. No one is locked up, and no one is punished but, according to workers there, 'we listen, listen, listen … we also challenge behaviour.'

The scheme is controversial – and expensive. But its supporters say that it works, while most youth detention centres don't – and having someone spend their life in and out of prison costs even more. 'Hassela gave me love and rules, and listened to me when I was sad. Most of my former friends in Stockholm are either dead or in jail,' says one former student.

ALTERNATIVES TO PRISON

It is better to try to help young people get 'back on the rails' than to concentrate on punishment. That is the view of most experts who work with troublesome – and troubled – youth. Because of this, there is often a greater emphasis on 'rehabilitation' (reform) with young offenders than there is with adults. Once someone has been through the criminal justice system, this becomes progressively more difficult.

Keeping out of court

Alternatives to court can include warnings (called cautions) from the police about what punishment certain criminal acts are likely to result in if they continue. Setting up counselling for young people who seem to have problems that make offending a risk, using family conferences to discuss problem behaviour and getting help for young people who have drug and alcohol problems are all helpful. If they work, it means the young person is spared the ordeal of a court appearance and the subsequent criminal record, which can have all kinds of damaging effects on their future.

After court

Once in court, there is a range of penalties available. For example, there are fines; 'community service' (when offenders have to spend a number of hours doing useful, unpaid work); and 'suspended sentences', which means a prison sentence that doesn't actually have to be served unless the offender commits another crime. A young person might also be put on probation, where he or she must report regularly to a probation officer to make sure they are staying out of trouble. In some countries, including the UK, a young person who has

▶ A young offender chats with his probation officer. Her job is to help the court decide on the best way to deal with offenders and to ensure that they carry out their sentence.

▲ *Young offenders in New York carry out 'community service' – cleaning the streets instead of being sent to a detention centre or prison.*

committed a serious offence may be told they must stay indoors after a certain time of night, and they may have to wear a radio-controlled monitoring device or tag that tells the police where they are at all times. However, tagging is controversial and some experts think it is not effective.

Better – and cheaper?

These punishments may sound harsh, but they do mean that a young person can stay in the community, in a safe place. This is important, because it is widely recognised that one of the main results of sending a young offender to prison is that he or she just learns how to be a better criminal. Avoiding prison sentences is also a lot cheaper for the government. Putting a young offender in prison costs around 12 times as much as other penalties.

ON TARGET

In the US, the term 'Youth Courts' does not refer to juvenile courts, but to a voluntary initiative, also called 'teen courts'. These allow non-violent young first offenders to be 'tried' by other young people (overseen by adult specialists). It is a way of bringing young people before a court, while keeping them away from 'hard-core' offenders and out of the adult court system.

PREVENTION IS BETTER THAN CURE

'It is better to build fences at the top of cliffs than provide ambulances at the bottom,' says criminologist Howard Williams. By this he means that it is better to try to stop a young person getting into the cycle of offending in the first place. But this cannot be done unless we make an effort to understand why young people get involved with crime, and help them to get out of it.

Danger signals

Lots of young people make one or two mistakes when they are young, but go on to live normal, happy, law-abiding lives. But other young people are always in trouble and are in danger of getting sucked into a bitter cycle of crime. These young people often have chaotic homes; their parents may be absent or for some other reason cannot give them the support and guidance they need. Such young people need extra help. If they are lucky, they may find a teacher or youth worker who can help them build up the strength and resilience that they will need to resist pressure to take dangerous, criminal routes in life.

BUSTED!

Steve nearly went to prison for driving without a licence, or any of the right papers, and being extremely drunk. But instead, he was ordered to do a year's community service and to wear a radio-controlled 'tag'. Steve was a failure at school, but he's now doing a course in business, and has plans to become a DJ and to set up a youth club. He is very glad not to be in jail. 'If I had gone to prison, I would have come out worse,' he says.

◄ Young mothers attend a parenting class. Teaching the skills needed to be a supportive and helpful parent can be hugely important in bringing up a new generation of young people.

▶ *Providing young people with structured activities and challenges can play an important part in helping them develop into stronger individuals.*

What to do?

Identifying troubled young people is crucial: challenging behaviour such as bullying, truanting and being disruptive are all signs that a young person may need help rather than punishment. Parents may need help and guidance in getting their own lives on track. Very often, they, too have chaotic and difficult backgrounds and do not know how to keep their children out of trouble. Whole communities may need help, such as programmes to help the very youngest children get a good start in their early years. After-school clubs, youth clubs and activities to keep teenagers occupied and challenged, and a range of other interventions can all also help. But perhaps the hardest task is also the most important one – helping young people to break away from the cycle of behaviour that they have grown up with.

And the police?

Sympathetic policing is vital. Where some people and communities seem to be more often in trouble than others, it is essential to find out if they are being treated fairly – and if not, to put things right. If there are reasons why they are in trouble so much, such as the breakdown of families, drink and drug problems, these have to be understood and addressed, rather than just heavy-handedly locking people up. It is a huge task, and not everything works for everyone – but it is essential that we keep trying.

ON TARGET

Helping young offenders who have just been released from custody is very important, as at this point, they may well be tempted back into crime. They need plenty of positive help and support. This is not always there, but it can be, sometimes. This is what a young man named Leroy told The Howard League for Penal Reform, a campaigning organisation concerned with prisons, about the help the social services had given him: 'They concentrated on getting me a job and … training … [They] kept me off the street and from mixing with my old friends and getting into badness.'

GLOSSARY

Abduction kidnapping, in particular that of a child.

Addictive Causing dependence (addiction). If you are addicted to a drug, you feel you cannot live without it.

Apartheid A system of racial segregation that was practised in South Africa in the second half of the 20th century.

Binge drinking A heavy drinking session that ends in drunkenness. Also called 'heavy episodic drinking'.

Borstal A type of youth custody in the United Kingdom, abolished in 1982 in favour of other forms of accommodation for young offenders.

Community service A punishment issued by a court that means the offender must perform useful work for the community.

Crime syndicate A group of gangsters running organised crime.

Criminal record A record of the crimes a person has committed.

Criminologist Someone who studies crime.

Crossfire Bullets flying this way and that.

Curfew A period of time when people are not allowed to leave their homes.

Domestic violence Also known as domestic abuse – when people within families hurt each other.

Drug A substance that is taken to make changes in a body: to heal it, to make it feel different in some way – or even to poison it.

Electrocute To harm or kill using electricity.

Exclude To force a student to leave school.

Exploit To make unfair use of for one's own advantage.

Heterosexual Having sexual feelings for a person of the opposite sex.

Homosexual Having sexual feelings for a person of the same sex.

Illegal downloading Downloading/file-sharing music, films etc without the permission of the owner of the 'copyright' (usually the person or organisation that made the original).

Industrialisation The development of large industries.

Industrial Revolution The growth of factory production that took place in Britain first, and then elsewhere, from about 1750 to about 1850.

Juvenile Young: a juvenile court is a court where young people are put on trial – they are called 'Youth Courts' in the UK.

Manslaughter The killing of a human being without intending to.

Offender Someone who has committed a crime.

Penalty A punishment, such a fine or a period in prison.

Prostitution Having sex for money. A prostitute is someone who has sex for money.

Psychiatric To do with the treatment of mental and emotional disorders. A psychiatrist is a doctor who treats mental and emotional disorders.

Reformatory A prison for young criminals or a reform school.

Resilience Being able to resist pressure and endure difficult situations.

Secure accommodation Accommodation in which someone is locked in, or prevented from leaving.

Soft drugs Drugs that are not physically addictive, such as marijuana.

Solitary confinement Keeping a prisoner by his or herself as a punishment.

Status symbol A possession that shows someone's wealth or social rank.

Transported Sent away to another country as a punishment for a crime.

Tsotsi Black street gang member in South Africa.

Unprotected sex Sex without a condom to protect from sexually transmitted diseases.

Vandalism Damaging things in the environment on purpose.

Youth courts In some countries, this means juvenile courts. In the US it means courts set up and run by young people.

FURTHER INFORMATION

Books

Jacqui Bailey, *Talk About Youth Crime*, Wayland 2011

Dirk Flint, *Inside Crime: Drug Crime*, Franklin Watts, 2010

Colin Hynson, *Inside Crime: Cybercrime*, Franklin Watts 2010

Sarah Levete, *Talk About Gangs and Knife Crime*, Wayland 2010

Sarah Levete, *Talk About Internet Crime*, Wayland 2011

Brooke Kinsella, *Why Ben? A Sister's Story of Heartbreak and Love for the Brother She Lost*, Pocket Books 2009

Films

The Loneliness of the Long-Distance-Runner
A 1962 film of the story of a young man in secure accommodation – 'borstal' – and how he got there.

Websites

www.thesite.org/homelawandmoney/law/introuble/youngoffenders
How young people are drawn into crime.

www.bbc.co.uk/schools/citizenx/national/crime/lowdown/crime_info_1.shtml and http://www.bbc.co.uk/schools/citizenx/national/crime/lowdown/crime_basics_2.shtml
Young people talk about crime.

www.howardleague.org
The website of the campaigning organisation 'The Howard League' which has published a number of booklets on crime and young people.

www.bbchistorymagazine.com/feature/youth-culture-and-crime-what-can-we-learn-history
A look at youth crime throughout history.

www.ias.org.uk
A downloadable pdf on Alcohol and Crime in the UK

www.cdc.gov/HealthyYouth/alcoholdrug/index.htm
Alcohol and illegal drug use among young Americans.

www.facebook.com/drugsnot4me
Canadian website on drugs.

www.ojjdp.gov/pubs/reform/ch2_e.html
Combating street gangs in the US.

news.bbc.co.uk/1/hi/world/africa/1910693.stm
Street children in South Africa talk about their lives.

www.ncjrs.gov/ovc_archives/bulletins/gun_7_2001/gun2_2_01.html
Gun crime in the US.

www.bbc.co.uk/worldservice/people/highlights/001109_child.shtml
Comparing two cases of children who killed.

news.bbc.co.uk/1/hi/world/americas/1203977.stm
Children and guns in the US.

www.hmcourts-service.gov.uk/infoabout/magistrates/youth.htm
About youth courts in the UK.

www.usatoday.com/news/health/2006-09-20-teen-crime_x.htm
Debating the use of adult prisons for young people.

www.rethinking.org.uk/facts/docs/alternatives_to_prison.pdf
Alternatives to prison.

www.abanet.org/publiced/tab26.pdf
About the US Teen Courts.

Note to parents and teachers: every effort has been made by the Publishers to ensure that these websites are suitable for children, that they are of the highest educational value, and that they contain no inappropriate or offensive material. However, because of the nature of the Internet, it is impossible to guarantee that the contents of these sites will not be altered. We strongly advise that Internet access is supervised by a responsible adult.

INDEX

abuse, child 16, 31
addiction 18–19, 20, 21
alcohol 8, 14, 15, 18-19, 36, 38, 40, 41
apartheid 24, 25

Bell, Mary 29, 30–31
borstals (UK) 36
breakdown, family 10, 11, 23, 24, 40, 41
Bulger, James 28, 29, 31
bullying 14, 26, 33, 36, 41

centres, detention 28, 35, 37, 39
consent, age of 16
convicts, transportation of 10
counselling 38
courts, juvenile/youth 11, 34-35, 38-39
crime, violent 8, 19, 22, 23, 24–25, 28–31, 32–33
criminologists 14, 23, 40

dealers, drug 12, 20, 21, 22
drink driving 18, 40
drinking, binge 18, 19
drugs 8, 14, 15, 18–21, 36, 37, 38, 41

education 9, 11, 15, 23, 25, 36, 37, 40
education, sex 17

fare-dodging 14

gangs, youth 22–25
graffiti 8
guns 22, 23, 26, 27, 32, 33

harassment (by police) 12, 13
Hassela Reform Centre 37
Heavenly Creatures 29
homosexuality 16
Howard League 41
Houses of Refuge 11

Industrial Revolution 10, 11, 28
institutes, young offender 36, 37

killers, child 28–31
knives 26, 27

manslaughter 29, 30
maras 23
marijuana 15, 20
massacres, school and college 32–33
Mercer, Sean 23
murder 8, 19, 22, 23, 28–31, 35
music, illegally downloading 14, 15

offences, public order 12, 13

parenting 23, 29, 31, 40, 41
penalty, death 20, 35
police 12, 13, 24, 25, 27, 30, 33, 38, 41
pregnancy, teen 17
prison 9, 11, 15, 20, 23, 25, 31, 35, 36, 37, 38, 39, 40, 41
probation 38
prostitution 10, 16

rape 16, 17
record, criminal 15, 37, 38
reformatories 9, 11
reformers, social 11, 16, 25
rehabilitation 36, 37, 38, 39
responsibility, age of criminal 9, 34
riots
    Australia 13
    Paris 13
robbery 8, 11, 22
'Romeo and Juliet Law' 17

schools, reform 11, 29, 31
sentencing 9, 35
service, community 14, 38, 39, 40
shoplifting 8, 14
South Africa 9, 24–25
Stead, William 16
stealing 8, 9, 10, 11, 14, 19, 22
stop and search 12, 13

tagging 39
transportation 10
tsotsis 24

vandalism 8

Walsh, David 33
Walters, George 11
weapons, carrying illegal 12, 22, 26–27
Weise, Jeff 32
welfare 34, 35
Williams, Howard 40
Witt, Tylar 35

SERIES CONTENTS

Cybercrime Hacking • Case study: Gary McKinnon • Phishing • Cyberbullying • Cyberstalking • Virus attacks • Malware • Social networking sites • Fraudulent websites • Denial-of-service attacks • Identity theft • Case study: Pirate Bay • Cyberterrorism • Cyberwars • Case study: Cyberwars in Eastern Europe • Cybersecurity

Drug crime Worldwide drug problem • Which drugs are illegal? • Who are the criminals? • The flow of drugs • The cost of drugs • Tackling the traffickers • Smuggling and mules • Below the waves • Stop and search • Global drug watch • Surveillance • Operation Junglefowl • Going undercover • Drug bust • Operation Habitat • Drugs on the street • The future of drug crime

Forensics The use of forensics • The history • Securing the crime scene • Using post-mortems • Looking at the evidence: insects • Soil and seeds • Blood • DNA evidence • Bones and skulls • Clothes and shoes • Forgeries • Guns and bullets • Narcotics • Crash investigations • Explosions • Forensics and ancient history

People trafficking Defining people trafficking • History of people trafficking • The traffickers • The victims • Forced labour • The sex industry • Trafficking children • Source countries • In transit • Border controls • Case study: The European Union • Catching the criminals • Loopholes in the law • Police and welfare • Working with NGOs • Raising awareness • Taking a stand

Gun crime Defining gun crime • Which guns are used? • Who commits gun crime? • Case study: killing spree • How much gun crime is there? • Gun dealing • Gun control • Arming the police • Case study: Ganglands • Solving gun crime • Firearms in the crime lab • Case study: Washington snipers • Combating gun crime • Operation Trident • Gun crime in the media • Firearms debate

Youth crime Inside picture • Changing times • 'Move along, please' • Everybody does it! • The problem with sex • The demon drink • Drugs and young people • Gangs • Case study: Youth gangs in South Africa • Armed and dangerous • Children who kill • Case study: Mary Bell • School and college massacres • On trial • 'Banged up' • Alternatives to prison • Prevention better than cure

Kidnapping and piracy Inside picture • In the past • Piracy at sea • Somalia • Case study: The MV Sirius Star • Policing the pirates • Prosecution and detention • Kidnapping for ransom • Abducting children • Taken hostage • Case study: Lebanon• Hijacking • Negotiation • Armed response • Case study: 9/11 • Training and support • Surviving kidnap and piracy

Policing and justice Criminal justice • Tackling crime • Officers on the street • National/international police • Police culture • Case study: police racism • Who guards the guardians? • Case study: A new police force • The justice system • Arrest and detention • The courts • Crime and punishment • Community sentences • Case study: terrorism • Victims • Young offenders • Changes to the system